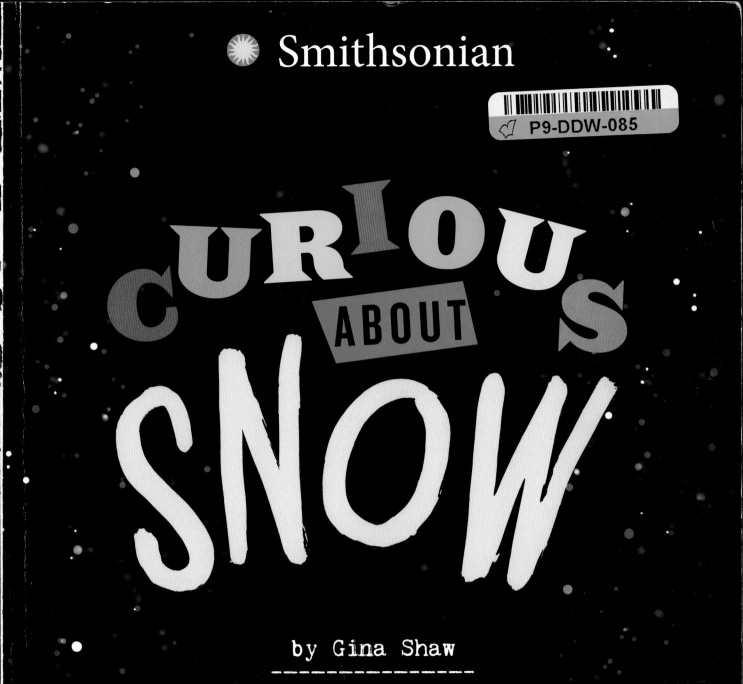

Smithsonian

CURIOUS ABOUT SNOW

by Gina Shaw

GROSSET & DUNLAP
An Imprint of Penguin Random House

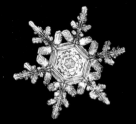

GROSSET & DUNLAP

Penguin Young Readers Group
An Imprint of Penguin Random House LLC

● Smithsonian

This trademark is owned by the Smithsonian Institution and
is registered in the U.S. Patent and Trademark Office.

Smithsonian Enterprises:
Christopher Liedel, President
Carol LeBlanc, Senior Vice President, Education and Consumer Products
Brigid Ferraro, Vice President, Education and Consumer Products
Ellen Nanney, Licensing Manager
Kealy Gordon, Product Development Manager

Smithsonian Institution, National Museum of Natural History:
Dr. Don E. Wilson, Curator Emeritus, Department of Vertebrate Zoology

PHOTO CREDITS: NASA/NOAA: 26. © **KENNETH LIBBRECHT:** 21, 23. **SMITHSONIAN INSTITUTION:**
front and back covers (large snowflakes), 9 (right), 13, 16–17, 18–19, 20, 22, 25 (bottom); 32.
SMITHSONIAN INSTITUTION ARCHIVES: 9 (left). **THINKSTOCK:** cover (background, photo by dmilovanovic),
3 (photo by Comstock), 4 (photo by saiva), 5 (photo by heckepics), 6–7 (photo by sam_eder), 8 (top, photo by rvika;
bottom, photo by 4maksym), 11 (photo by vermontalm), 12 (top, photo by scottrichmond_pix; lower left, photo by CathyDoi;
lower right, photo by saiva), 24 (photo by Dainis Derics), 25 (top, photo by Aquir), 26 (upper left, photo by Peter Spiro),
27 (photo by Lysogor), 30 (top, photo by Svetaleo; bottom, photo by Jupiterimages), 31 (top, photo by og-vision; bottom,
photo by Ariel Skelley). **WILSON BENTLEY DIGITAL ARCHIVES OF THE JERICHO HISTORICAL SOCIETY/
SNOWFLAKEBENTLEY.COM:** 10, 14, 15 (top and bottom).

Library of Congress Cataloging-in-Publication Data is available.

ISBN 978-0-448-49018-2   10 9 8 7 6 5 4 3 2 1

Have you ever built a snow fort? Or tossed snowballs? Or caught a snowflake on your tongue? Or wished you could try this where you live?

SNOW

often makes people stop what they're doing to watch it fall from the sky. But what is snow and how is it formed?

To snow, the temperature must be below 32°F (Fahrenheit) or 0°C (Celsius), the freezing point of water. Water vapor, a gas that is produced when water evaporates, sticks to a cold speck inside a cloud and makes it wet. This speck can be a particle of soil or salt left over from ocean water that evaporated. It can be pollen from a flower or ash from a volcano, among other things.

Inside the cloud, more water vapor sticks to the wet speck and forms a water droplet. This droplet freezes into a ball of ice, and more water vapor sticks to it.

The ball of ice begins to grow into a **hexagon**-shaped ice crystal.

Water vapor sticks to the crystal's six corners first since they stick out farther than any other part of the crystal. As the six corners grow and push outward, they begin to form arms. This process is called branching.

Branches on the six corners begin to sprout. The new branches keep growing and form little arms of their own.

Soon, an amazing snow crystal forms. To scientists, snowflakes and snow crystals are the same thing.

The snow crystal keeps growing as it falls through the cloud. The size of the snowflake depends on how many ice crystals connect together.
An average-size snowflake is usually made up of about 200 ice crystals and 180 billion molecules of water!

The shape of the snowflake is determined by the temperature and humidity of the air. The colder the air temperature, the sharper the tips of the snow crystal will be. At warmer temperatures, snow crystals grow slower, and their shapes are less sharp. Snow crystals usually form simpler shapes when the humidity is low, and more complex shapes when it is high.

When a snowflake becomes heavy enough, it falls through the cloud to the ground. It continues to grow and change as it falls toward the earth.

If the ground is cold enough, the snowflake will stick to it and won't melt right away.

How do we know as much as we do about snowflakes?

A man named Wilson A. Bentley loved snow so much he studied it for most of his life. Bentley was born on February 9, 1865.

Wilson A. Bentley

He grew up and worked on his family farm in Jericho, Vermont, in the heart of the **snow belt**. The yearly snowfall in Jericho was about 120 inches. It was a perfect place to learn about snow!

As a young boy, Bentley enjoyed studying the world around him: from butterflies, leaves, and spiderwebs to weather conditions, raindrops, and snowflakes. Bentley loved catching single snowflakes and studying them.

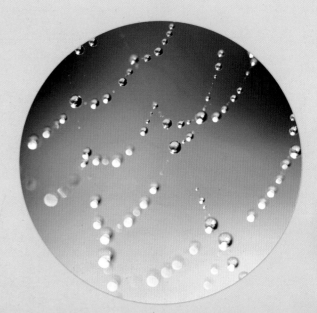

Bentley's mother gave him an old microscope for his fifteenth birthday. Looking at snowflakes through his microscope, he was amazed by the beautiful crystals—and by how many different types of snowflakes he found.

For three winters, Bentley drew one hundred snowflakes a year. But the snow crystals always melted before he could finish drawing them. This was very frustrating to him.

When Bentley turned seventeen, his parents bought him a **bellows** camera and a new microscope. He attached the microscope to the camera and spent the next two years trying to photograph snowflakes.

Snowflakes are very difficult to photograph because they melt so quickly. But, finally, on January 15, 1885, when he was nineteen years old, Bentley became the first person ever to photograph a single snowflake! He then went on to capture more than five thousand images of snow crystals.

Bentley as an adult taking pictures of snowflakes

Because of his amazing work, he became known as the "Snowflake Man" and was also often called "Snowflake" Bentley.

Many colleges and universities around the world bought Bentley's snow-crystal photographs. He published about sixty articles in magazines and journals. His book *Snow Crystals* was published in 1931, the same year that he died.

Snow Crystals contained more than 2,400 photographs. Bentley wanted people to be able to study and enjoy his snowflake photographs. His mission was to record something that disappeared very quickly.

Wilson Bentley proved that snowflakes had different shapes, but almost all had six sides.

Star-shaped snowflakes are called stellar dendrites. They have six arms that branch out from a center point. The center point is the speck that started the crystal. These snow crystals form when the temperature is about 5°F, or -15°C. This shape is the one most people think of as a snowflake.

stellar dendrites

Hexagonal-plate snowflakes don't have arms. The points are the beginnings of arms that were just starting to develop when the crystal fell out of its cloud and stopped growing. These snowflakes form when the temperature is near 28°F (-2°C) or near 5°F (-15°C). Sometimes a star pattern can be seen in the center of a hexagonal plate.

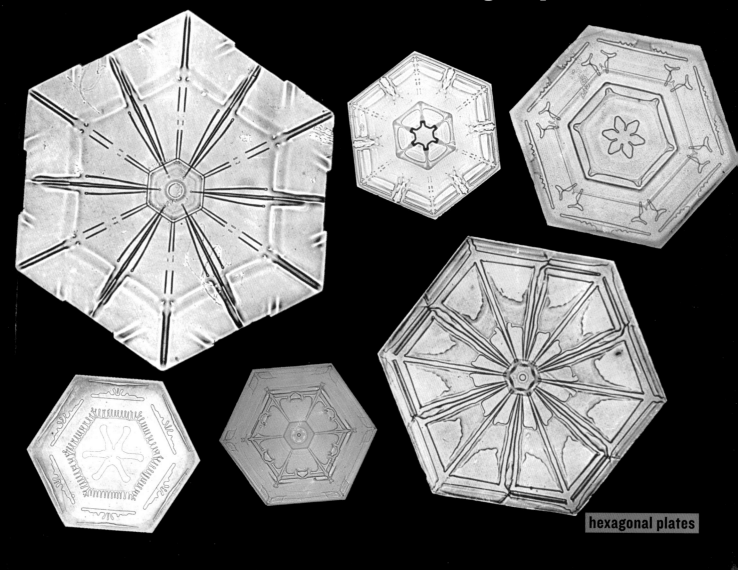

hexagonal plates

Modern scientists and photographers have continued Wilson Bentley's work. Their photographs, like his, tell us more about different snowflakes.

stellar plates

A stellar plate is a snowflake whose shape fans out like a star. Stellar plates may have bumps or simple arms without branches. They are more common than hexagonal-plate snowflakes.

Needles are very thin snow crystals. They may be solid, hollow, or partly hollow. They grow when the temperature is about 23°F (-5°C).

needles

Column snow crystals have six sides. These crystals can be solid, hollow, or capped. They can be short and squat or long and thin.

hollow column

capped column

Column snowflakes form very high in the clouds and at very cold temperatures. They are tiny. Snow crystals that fall as columns make for very slippery snow!

It is highly unlikely that any two snowflakes ever look the same. They all form in their own way even though they start out with the same structure. So much can happen as a snow crystal falls to the earth. For example, if a water droplet passes close to one arm, that arm might grow faster. Soon, that arm will be a lot longer than the others. For this reason, most snowflakes are not perfect. They may grow unevenly, break, melt and refreeze, or come in contact with other crystals.

imperfect snowflakes

A snow crystal might be a twin. It can have twelve arms. This happens when two ice crystals start from one speck and form on top of each other.

a twin snowflake

a snow crystal with rime

Some snowflakes have little bumps on them. These bumps are called rime. Sometimes water droplets strike the crystal and freeze on contact. This causes rime.

As pretty as snowflakes can be, snow can be dangerous. Heavy snow can strand drivers, block deliveries, and disrupt emergency services. Buildings can collapse under the weight of too much snow. Trees and power lines can come down.

Here are some winter storms to watch out for.

A snowstorm is a storm with a large amount of falling snow. Billions of snowflakes fall in every snowstorm.

During a thundersnow, thunder rumbles and lightning flashes. Sometimes as much as two inches of snow per hour will fall.

Blizzards are snowstorms that contain large amounts of snow or blowing snow. Winds are usually more than thirty-five miles an hour. **Visibility** is less than a quarter mile. A blizzard continues for more than three hours.

An avalanche, also called a snowslide, is a moving mass of snow that slides down a mountain. It may contain ice, soil, rocks, and uprooted trees. The avalanche moves faster and becomes more powerful as it gets closer to the bottom of the slope. This can cause even the smallest avalanche to be a major disaster.

Avalanche!

Snowflakes and snowstorms can set records! Here are some snow facts by the numbers.

One inch of rain equals about 6 inches (15 cm) of heavy, wet snow, or 12 inches (30 cm) of very light, puffy snow.

The average snowflake measures about 1/2 inch (1.27 cm). You need a magnifying glass to see its shape. Some of the largest snowflakes range from 3 to 4 inches (8 to 10 cm) in length.

According to *Guinness World Records*, the world's largest snowflake fell in 1887 in Fort Keogh, Montana. This snowflake was 15 inches wide (38 cm) and 8 inches thick (20 cm).

About 12% of Earth's land surface is covered with snow and ice.

The most snow to fall in 1 day (24 hours) was 6 feet (2 m) in Silver Lake, Colorado, in 1921.

Stampede Pass, Washington, is the snowiest place in the United States. It gets about 36 feet (11 m) of snow a year.

The most snowfall over the course of a year was at Mount Rainier, Washington. It snowed 94 feet (29 m) from February 19, 1971, through February 19, 1972.

People around the world celebrate winter and the snow it brings with winter festivals.

Kids like to celebrate, too. Wherever there's snow, you'll see somebody rolling and shaping it to build a snowperson. Or digging through it to build a snow cave. Or whooshing down a hill on a sled, snow tube, snowboard, or skis.

What is your favorite snow activity?

bellows: the pleated part of a camera that can be expanded

droplet: a very small bit of liquid

evaporate: to change from a liquid into a gas

hexagon: a shape with six straight sides

humidity: the amount of moisture in the air

molecule: the smallest bit of a particular kind of material that has all the same qualities as that material

snow belt: a region that receives a large amount of snowfall yearly

visibility: the ability to see

water vapor: the gas that is produced when water evaporates